Basic Environment Topics To Prepare for UPSC-CSE

Phosphorus Cycle

Phosphorus plays a central role in aquatic ecosystems and water quality.

Unlike carbon and nitrogen, which come primarily from the atmosphere, **phosphorus occurs in large amounts as a mineral in phosphate rocks** and enters the cycle from erosion and mining activities.

This is the nutrient considered to be the **main cause of excessive growth of rooted and free-floating microscopic plants (phytoplankton) in lakes (which leads to eutrophication).**

The main storage for phosphorus is in the earth's crust. On land, phosphorus is usually found in the form of phosphates. Through the process of weathering and erosion, phosphates enter rivers, streams and finally oceans. In the ocean, phosphorus accumulates on continental shelves in the form of insoluble deposits.

The difference between the carbon and phosphorous cycle is:

- There is no respiratory release of phosphorus into the atmosphere like carbon.
- Atmospheric inputs of phosphorus through rainfall are much smaller than carbon inputs.
- Gaseous exchanges of phosphorus between organism and environment are negligible.

The Evergreen Rainforest

- **This biome extends upto 100 latitudes on both sides of the equator**. It covers the area of the Amazon lowland of South America, the Congo basin of equatorial Africa and the South-Eastern Asian Islands extending from Sumatra to New Guinea
- This area experiences high temperatures throughout the year with **ranges of as little as 2°C**. However, the daily range of temperature is much higher than the annual range of temperature.
- This area gets **heavy rainfall ranging between 150cm-250cm**. It is distributed throughout the year. Rainfall occurs in the afternoon almost on daily basis.
- The combination of heat and moisture makes this biome a perfect environment for a great variety of plants and animal species. The variety of plant species can be understood from the fact that one square kilometre may contain as many as about a thousand different types of plant species. **Most of the trees have buttressed trunks, shallow roots and large dark evergreen leaves.**

Temperate Grassland Biome

- Temperate grasslands are located in two typical locations i.e. the **interior of the continent in the northern hemisphere and the margin of the continents in the southern hemisphere.**

- The temperate grasslands of the northern hemisphere are characterized by a continental climate wherein extremes of summer and winter temperatures are well marked. **Though grasslands in the southern hemisphere are located along the coast, these are located in the**

rain shadow areas of the high coastal mountains. These locations account for scanty rainfall in all these regions.

- These grasslands are found on all the continents under different names. In the northern hemisphere, the grasslands are far more extensive. **In Eurasia, they are called the steppes** and stretch eastwards from the shores of the Black Sea to the plains of Manchuria in China. **In North America, the grasslands are quite extensive and they are called prairies.** They lie between the foothills of the Rockies and the Great Lakes. **In the southern hemisphere, these grasslands are less extensive. These are known as Pampas in Argentina and Uruguay. In South Africa, these grasslands are sandwiched** between Drakensberg Mountains and the Kalahari Desert **and are called veldt. In Australia, these grasslands are known as Downs** and are found in the Murray – Darling basins of South Australia.

- The majority of the grasslands have been converted into agricultural lands which have now become famous **'granaries of the world'.**

Podzols

Podzols are the typical soils of a **coniferous or boreal biome.**

The **top layer of the soil is very thin** and overlain over a sandy or loamy subsurface which has **no organic matter** (lost due to leaching of nutrients to the bottom layers).

The soils are **characterized by low levels of moisture** (excessively drained) and nutrients and are loamy or sandy. **Others have shallow** rooting zones and poor drainage due to subsoil cementation.

A low pH further compounds the issue. The low pH (acidic) is due to **excessive leaching of alkaline matter** which if present would neutralise the organic acids of the accumulating litter.

Hence, most **Podzols are poor soils for agriculture.** They are **mostly used for grazing.**

Air Independent Propulsion Technology

The Air Independent Propulsion Technology is **developed by the Naval Materials Research Laboratory (NMRL) of DRDO.**

Key features are:

- The Air Propulsion System **allows the submarines to stay for long hours in water.** The submarines need to come to the surface of the water to charge their batteries. This is reduced by Air Propulsion System.
- It **decreases the noise levels made by the submarines while travelling.** This makes it hard to detect the submarines.
- It is a **fuel-cell based Air Propulsion System.**
- It uses a **Phosphoric Acid Fuel Cell.**

The system was **developed under the Atma Nirbhar Bharat Campaign.** Currently, this technology is available only in France, the US, the UK, China and Russia.

Temperature Inversion

*Temperature inversion is a reversal of the normal behaviour of temperature in the **troposphere**, in which a **layer of cool air at the surface is overlain by a layer of warmer air.***

Favourable Conditions for velocity and direction of the wind are the net result of the wind generating forces.

The winds in the upper atmosphere, 2 – 3 km above the surface, are free from the frictional effect of the surface and are controlled by the pressure gradient and the Coriolis force.

Hadley cell: The cell is **located between 10- 30-degree latitude in both the hemisphere**. This is a *thermally induced cell and is the result of intense solar insolation*. The intense insolation produces rising air along the equator. The rising air cools down below tropopause and diverges towards the pole as anti-trade. They lead to upper air pilation around 30 degrees latitude and sink causing the sub-tropical high pressure. The trade wind flows from this HP toward the equator and completes this cell. It is one of the most permanent cells and is associated with Tropical monsoon climate and tropical desert.

Ferrell Cell: In the middle latitudes the circulation is that of sinking cold air that comes from the poles and the rising warm air that blows from the subtropical high. At the surface, these winds are called westerlies and the cell is known as the Ferrel cell.

Temperature Inversion is:

- **Long winter nights**: Loss of heat by terrestrial radiation from the ground surface during the night may exceed the amount of incoming solar radiation.
- **Cloudless and clear sky:** Loss of heat through terrestrial radiation proceeds more rapidly without any obstruction.

- **Dry air near the ground surface**: It limits the absorption of the radiated heat from the Earth's surface.
- **The slow movement of air**: It results in no transfer or mixing of heat in the lower layers of the atmosphere.
- **Snow-covered ground surface**: It results in a maximum loss of heat through the reflection of incoming solar radiation.

General Circulation of Atmosphere

The velocity and direction of the wind are the net results of the wind generating forces.

The winds in the upper atmosphere, 2 – 3 km above the surface, are free from the frictional effect of the surface and are controlled by the pressure gradient and the Coriolis force.

Hadley cell: The cell is **located between 10- 30-degree latitude in both the hemisphere**. This is a *thermally induced cell and is the result of intense solar insolation.* The intense insolation produces rising air along the equator. The rising air cools down below tropopause and diverges towards the pole as anti-trade. They lead to upper air pilation around 30 degrees latitude and sink causing the sub-tropical high pressure. The trade wind flows from this HP toward the equator and completes this cell. It is one of the most permanent cells and is associated with Tropical monsoon climate and tropical desert.

Ferrell Cell: In the middle latitudes the circulation is that of sinking cold air that comes from the poles and the rising warm air that blows from the subtropical high. At the surface, these winds are called westerlies and the cell is known as the Ferrel cell.

Jet Streams

Jet streams are fast-moving currents of air that circulate above the Earth. When people refer to "the jet stream" they are usually referring to the polar-front jet stream or the subtropical jet stream, two major jet streams that shape weather patterns around the world.

Jet streams travel in the tropopause—the area between the troposphere and the stratosphere—at **heights of about 8 to 15 kilometres.**

Jet streams are **stronger in winter in the northern and southern hemispheres**, because that's when air temperature differences that drive them to tend to be most pronounced.

The polar-front jet stream forms at about 60 degrees latitude in both hemispheres, **while the subtropical jet stream forms at about 30 degrees.**

Air north of a jet stream is typically colder, while air to the south is usually warmer. As jet streams dip or break off, they move air masses around, creating shifts in global weather patterns.

Rising global temperatures from global warming are affecting the jet stream and, in turn, the weather. Because the Earth's polar regions are warming more quickly than the rest of the world, the temperature contrast that drives jet streams has decreased. **Slower, weaker jet streams have been linked to melting in Greenland and a potential rise in deadly weather events because they can lock weather systems into place, stalling them over regions.**

Dew point, Relative and Specific Humidity

Dew Point: The air containing moisture to its full capacity at a given temperature is said to be saturated. It means that the air at the given temperature is incapable of holding any additional amount of moisture at that stage. The temperature at which saturation occurs in a given sample of air is known as the dew point. **Dew point occurs when Relative Humidity is 100%.**

Relative Humidity: The *percentage of moisture present in the atmosphere* as compared to its full capacity at a given temperature is known as relative humidity.

The relative humidity is greater over the Oceans and least over the Continents. It determines the amount and rate of evaporation and hence it is an important climatic factor.

Air containing moisture to its full capacity at a given temperature is said to be 'saturated'. At this temperature, the air cannot hold any additional amount of moisture. Thus, the relative humidity of the saturated air is 100%.

Specific Humidity: It is expressed as the **weight of water vapour per unit weight of air**. Since it is measured in units of weight (usual grams per kilogram), the specific humidity is not affected by changes in pressure or temperature.

The Polar Vortex

The polar vortex is a <u>**large area of low pressure and cold air surrounding both of the Earth's poles**</u>. It always **exists near the poles, but weakens in summer and strengthens in winter.**

The polar Vortex is not something that will be visibly observed like tornadoes; funnel clouds, thunderstorms, lightning etc.

Features:

- The polar vortex spins in the stratosphere.
- Usually, when the vortex is strongest, cold air is less likely to plunge deep into North America or Europe. In other words, it forms a wall that protects the mid-latitudes from cold Arctic air.
- But occasionally, the polar vortex is disrupted and weakens, due to wave energy propagating upward from the lower atmosphere. When this happens, the stratosphere warms sharply in an event known as sudden stratospheric warming, in just a few days, miles above the Earth's surface.
- The warming weakens the polar vortex, shifting its location somewhat south of the pole or, in some instances, 'splitting' the vortex up into 'sister vortices'.

Sudden stratospheric warming also leads to the warm Arctic not only in the stratosphere but also in the troposphere as well. A warmer Arctic, in turn, favours more severe winter weather in the Northern Hemisphere middle latitudes including the eastern US.

Heat Wave

A Heat Wave is a period of **abnormally high temperatures**, more than the normal maximum temperature that occurs during the summer season. Heat Waves typically occur between March and June, and in some rare cases even extend till July.

Criteria for Heat Waves:

The Indian Meteorological Department (IMD) has given the following criteria for Heat Waves:

- Heat Waves need not be considered till the **maximum temperature of a station reaches at least 40°C for Plains and at least 30°C for Hilly regions.**
- **When the normal maximum temperature of a station is less than or equal to 40°C, Heat Wave Departure from normal is 5°C to 6°C and Severe Heat Wave Departure from normal is 7°C or more.**
- **When the normal maximum temperature of a station is more than 40°C, Heat Wave Departure from normal is 4°C to 5°C and Severe Heat Wave Departure from normal is 6°C or more.**
- **When the actual maximum temperature remains 45°C or more irrespective of the normal maximum temperature, heat waves should be declared.**

The magnified effect of paved and concrete surfaces in urban areas and a lack of tree cover known as urban heat island effects can make ambient temperatures feel 3 to 4 degrees more than they are is the cause of heatwaves in India.

Smog

Smog is the term derived from two words smoke and fog. It is a kind of intense air pollution. Smog is the result of the reaction of emissions from automobiles, factories, and industries with the sunlight and atmosphere.

The causes behind the formation of the smogs are different. Hence they are classified into 2 different types.

- **Photochemical Smog (Also called Los Angeles Smog)**
- **Sulfurous smog (Also called London Smog)**

Photochemical smog:

- Photochemical smog is created when **Sunlight reacts with Nitrogen oxide (NOx) and at least one Volatile Organic Compound** (VOC) in the atmosphere. This kind of smog requires neither smoke nor fog.
- Photochemical smog is **formed during the month of summer** in the afternoon when there is bright sunlight so that photochemical reactions can take place.
- **Ground-level ozone is the byproduct of this smog**. Ground-level ozone is not emitted directly into the atmosphere. It results from **photochemical reactions between oxides of nitrogen (NOx) and volatile organic compounds (VOCs) in the presence of sunlight.**

Sulfurous Smog:

- Sulfurous Smog is the result of a **high concentration of sulfur oxides in the atmosphere**. This is usually caused by the burning of fossil fuels like coal.
- **Sulfurous smog is also called "London smog," (first formed in London).**

Temperate Cyclones

Temperate cyclones are Confined to 350 – 650 N and S of the equator. More pronounced in the Northern hemisphere due to greater temperature contrast.

They have a dynamic origin and cyclone formation is due to frontogenesis (interaction of cold and warm fronts). When the warm-humid air masses from the tropics meet the dry-cold air masses from the poles and thus a polar front is formed as a surface of discontinuity. The cold air pushes the warm air upwards from underneath. Thus, a void is created because of the lessening of pressure. The surrounding air rushed in to occupy this void and coupled with the earth's rotation, a temperate cyclone is formed.

Temperate cyclones can originate on both landmass and water while tropical cyclones form only on seas with temperatures more than 26-270 C. They dissipate on reaching the land.

In a temperate cyclone, associated weather conditions are the mild and overcast sky in the initial stage and followed by moderate to heavy rain for a long period in a large area. So, here less destruction is due to winds but more destruction is due to flooding.

Tropical Cyclone

A tropical cyclone is a **rapidly rotating storm system characterized by a low-pressure centre, a closed low-level atmospheric circulation, strong winds, and a spiral arrangement of thunderstorms that produce heavy rain and/or squalls.**

Cyclones in the Bay of Bengal can be attributed to the vast low pressure created by the warm water of the ocean. The Bay of Bengal gets more rainfall with sluggish winds and warm air currents around it that keep temperatures relatively high all year. **The constant inflow of fresh warm water from the perineal rivers like the Brahmaputra, and Ganga makes it further impossible to mix with the cooler water below.**

As for the Arabian Sea, it is much calm as the stronger winds help dissipate the heat and the lack of constant fresh water helps the warm water mix with the cool water underneath, reducing the surface temperature.

The Bay of Bengal is shaped like a trough that makes it more hospitable for storms to gain force.

The lack of landmass between the Pacific Ocean and the Bay of Bengal tend cyclonic winds to move into the coastal areas causing heavy rainfall. **The Arabian Sea enjoys the locational advantage as the winds from the Pacific Ocean encounter the Western Ghats and the Himalayas cutting down on its intensity and sometimes never reaching the Arabian Sea.**

Tropical cyclones are violent storms that originate over oceans in tropical areas and move over to the coastal areas bringing about large scale destruction caused by violent winds, very heavy rainfall and storm surges.

Tropical cyclones originate and intensify over warm tropical oceans. The conditions favourable for the formation and intensification of tropical storms are:

- **Large sea surface with a temperature higher than 27° C.**
- **Presence of the Coriolis force.**
- **Small variations in the vertical wind speed.**
- **A pre-existing weak low-pressure area or low-level cyclonic circulation.**
- **Upper divergence above the sea level system.**

They originate in two distinct latitude zones, between 4° and 22° S and between 4° and 35° N. They are absent in the equatorial zone between 4° S and 4° N because of the absence of Coriolis force.

The Walker Circulation (Walker Cell)

The Walker circulation (walker cell) is **caused by the pressure gradient force that results from a high-pressure system over the eastern Pacific Ocean, and a low-pressure system over Indonesia.** The Walker cell is indirectly related to upwelling off the coasts of Peru and Ecuador. This brings nutrient-rich cold water to the surface, increasing fishing stocks.

In an El-Niño year, air pressure drops over large areas of the central Pacific and along the coast of South America.

The normal low-pressure system is replaced by a weak high in the western Pacific (the southern oscillation). **These changes in pressure patterns cause the trade winds to be reduced. This weakens the walker cell sometimes Walker Cell might even get reversed.**

This reduction allows the equatorial counter-current (current along with doldrums) to accumulate warm ocean water along the coastlines of Peru and Ecuador. This accumulation of warm water causes the thermocline to drop in the eastern part of the Pacific Ocean which cuts off the upwelling of cold deep ocean water along the coast of Peru.

Climatically, the development of an El Niño brings drought to the western Pacific, rains to the equatorial coast of South America, and convective storms and hurricanes to the central Pacific. Severe droughts occur in Australia, Indonesia, India and southern Africa.

Kelp Forests

Kelp Forests are **underwater ecosystems** formed in shallow water by the dense growth of several different species known as kelps.

Kelps are extremely large brown algae, although they look like plants.

They are underwater forests that thrive well in cold, nutrient-rich waters. Kelp forests have been observed throughout the Arctic and the Canadian Arctic alone represents 10 per cent of the world's coastlines.

Kelp attaches to the seafloor and eventually grows to the water's surface and relies on sunlight to generate food and energy.

The productive kelp forests tend to be associated with areas of significant oceanographic upwelling.

They are known for their high growth rate. Some varieties grow as fast as half a metre a day, **ultimately reaching 30 to 80 metres.**

Sea urchins can destroy entire kelp forests by moving in herds whereas Sea otters play a key role in stabilizing Sea urchin populations so that kelp forests may thrive.

LOTUS-HR

The local Treatment of Urban Sewage Streams for Healthy Reuse (LOTUS-HR) program aims to demonstrate a novel holistic (waste) water management approach that will produce clean water which can be reused for various purposes. The LOTUS-HR project is jointly supported by the *Department of Biotechnology, Ministry of Science and Technology, Government of India and Netherlands Organization for Scientific Research /STW, Government of Netherlands.*

iND-cepi & UMMID

- Ind-CEPI **(Coalition for Epidemic Preparedness Innovations)** Mission aims to strengthen the development of vaccines for the diseases of epidemic potential in India as well as build coordinated preparedness in the Indian public health system and vaccine industry to address existing and emerging infectious threats in India.

- UMMID **(Unique Methods of Management and Treatment of Inherited Disorders)** initiative aims to tackle inherited genetic diseases of newborn babies. The programme is implemented through government hospitals to regularise the use of cutting edge scientific technology and molecular medicine to achieve Universal Health Coverage for all. The initiative is

BBX11 Gene

Recently, the Indian Institute of Science Education and Research (IISER) has recognized the BBX11 gene that facilitates the **greening of crops.**

BBX11 plays a vital role in the regulation of the amount of protochlorophyllide synthesized by the plant.

- Protochlorophyllide is an intermediate in the synthesis of chlorophyll.
- If it is less, plants are unable to efficiently green to harvest sunlight and if the amount of protochlorophyllide is more, then photobleaching occurs.
- Photobleaching is the loss of colour by a pigment.
- The quantity of protochlorophyllide synthesised needs to be proportional to the variety of enzymes available to transform them into chlorophyll.
- It is very important to regulate the amount of protochlorophyllide synthesized by the plant.
- Chlorophyll is the green pigment in plants, algae, and cyanobacteria that absorbs sunlight and uses its energy to synthesise carbohydrates from carbon dioxide (CO_2) and water.

This discovery has many implications within the agriculture sector in tropical nations like India and can assist present results in optimising plant progress infrequently changing weather conditions.

GEAC and the GM crops

In India, the Genetic Engineering Appraisal Committee (GEAC) is the apex body that allows for the commercial release of GM crops.

The Genetic Engineering Appraisal Committee (GEAC) is a **statutory body** constituted under the **'Rules for the Manufacture, Use /Import /Export and Storage of Hazardous Microorganisms/Genetically Engineering Organisms or Cells, 1989' notified under the Environment (Protection) Act, 1986. It functions under the Ministry of Environment, Forests & Climate Change.**

Use of the _unapproved GM variant can attract a jail term of 5 years and a fine of Rs. 1 lakh under the Environment Protection Act, 1986._

The task of regulating GMO levels in imported consumables was initially with Genetic Engineering Appraisal Committee (GEAC) under the Union environment ministry. **Its role in this was diluted with the enactment of the Food Safety and Standards Act, 2006 and FSSAI was asked to take over approvals of imported goods.**

Nano Urea Liquid

Indian Farmers Fertiliser Cooperative Limited (IFFCO) introduced the world's first Nano Urea Liquid for farmers across the world.

It is a nutrient (liquid) to provides nitrogen to plants as an alternative to conventional urea.

It is developed to replace conventional urea and it can curtail the requirement of the same by at least 50%. Conventional urea is effective 30-40% in delivering nitrogen to plants, while the effectiveness of the Nano Urea Liquid is over 80%.

It has been found effective and efficient for plant nutrition which increases the production with improved nutritional quality.

It will boost a balanced nutrition program by reducing the excess use of Urea application in the soil and will make the crops stronger, and healthier and protect them from lodging effect. **Lodging is the bending over of the stems near ground level of grain crops, which makes them very difficult to harvest, and can dramatically reduce yield.**

Xenobiotics

Xenobiotics are **developed from stem cells of frogs.**

Xenobiotics, **named after the African clawed frog is synthetic organisms that are automatically designed by computers** to perform some desired function and built by combining different biological tissues.

They **could be made from a human patient's cells**, which would bypass the immune response challenges of other kinds of micro-robotic delivery systems.

Such xenobiotics could potentially be used to scrape plaque from arteries and with additional cell types and bioengineering, locate and treat disease.

They can also be _used for searching out nasty compounds or radioactive contamination and gathering microplastic in the oceans._

Seaweeds

They are the primitive, marine non-flowering marine algae without roots, stems and leaves, which play a major role in marine ecosystems.

The seaweeds derive nutrition through photosynthesis of sunlight and nutrients present in seawater. They release oxygen through every part of their bodies.

Importance of seaweeds:

They also **act as bio-indicator**. When waste from agriculture, industries, aquaculture and households is let into the ocean, it causes nutrient imbalance leading to algal blooming, a sign of marine chemical damage.

These aquatic organisms heavily **rely on iron for photosynthesis**. When the quantity of this mineral exceeds healthy levels and becomes dangerous to marine life, seaweeds trap it and prevent damage. Similarly, most heavy metals found in marine ecosystems are trapped and removed by seaweeds.

Seaweed has a **significant role in mitigating climate change**. By afforesting 9 per cent of the ocean with seaweed, it is possible to sequester 53 billion tons of carbon dioxide annually. Hence, there is a proposal termed **'ocean afforestation'** for farming seaweed to remove carbon.

There are **many species of blue-green algae** capable of fixing atmospheric nitrogen in the soil and are used as biofertilizers. **Common examples are Anabaena and Nostic.**
Anabaena, in association with water fern Azolla contributes nitrogen and also enriches soils with organic matter.

Indian Ocean Dipole (IOD)

The Indian Ocean Dipole (IOD) is defined by the difference in sea surface temperature between two areas (or poles, hence a dipole) **– a western pole in the Arabian Sea (western Indian Ocean) and an eastern pole in the eastern Indian Ocean south of Indonesia.**

IOD <u>develops in the equatorial region of the Indian Ocean from April to May peaking in October.</u>

With a positive IOD winds over the Indian Ocean blow from east to west (from the Bay of Bengal towards the Arabian Sea). This resulted in the Arabian Sea (the western Indian Ocean near Africa Coast) being much warmer and the eastern Indian Ocean around Indonesia becoming colder and dry.

<u>In the negative dipole year (negative IOD), the reverse happens to make Indonesia much warmer and rainier.</u>

<u>Positive IOD (Arabian Sea warmer than the Bay of Bengal) results in more cyclones than usual in the Arabian Sea.</u>

Global Environment Facility (GEF)

The Global Environment Facility (GEF) was **established on the eve of the 1992 Rio Earth Summit** to help tackle our planet's most pressing environmental problems. **The GEF unites 184 countries** in partnership with international institutions, Civil Society Organizations (CSOs), and the private sector to address global environmental issues while supporting national sustainable development initiatives.

The objectives of the Global Environment Facility are:

- **Strategically focusing its investments to catalyze transformational change in key systems that are driving major environmental loss, in particular energy, cities and food;**
- **Prioritizing integrated projects and programs that address more than one global environmental problem at a time, building on the GEF's unique position and mandate to act on a wide range of global environmental issues; and**
- **Implementing new strategies and policies to enhance results, including stronger engagement with the private sector, indigenous peoples, and civil society, and an increased focus on gender equality.**

The GEF runs a Small Grants Programme that provides financial and technical support to projects which embody a community-based approach. The GEF sees community-based projects as the cornerstone for addressing local and global environmental and sustainable development challenges.

Sea Cucumbers

They are marine animals with leathery skin and an elongated body containing a single, branched gonad. Sea cucumbers are **found on the seafloor worldwide.**

Sea cucumbers live chiefly among corals but are also found among rocks and in muddy and sandy flats. They are distributed from the shore to the great depths of oceans.

In India, the sea cucumber is **protected under Schedule I of the Wildlife Protection Act, 1972,** according to which the sea cucumbers cannot be transported for commercial use. In 2002, the Environmental Ministry of India banned the commercial harvesting of sea cucumbers.

The Dr KK Mohammed Koya Conservation Reserve is the **first sea cucumber conservation area in the world. It is located in the Cheriyapani Reef in the Union Territory of Lakshadweep. It was formed in 2020. It covers an area of 239 sq. km.**

Montreux Record

The Montreux Record is a register of wetland sites on the List of Ramsar wetlands of international importance where changes in ecological character have occurred, are occurring, or are likely to occur as a result of technological developments, pollution or other human interference.

It is a voluntary mechanism to highlight specific wetlands of international importance that are facing immediate challenges. It is maintained as part of the List of Ramsar wetlands of international importance. At present, 48 sites are listed in Montreux Record.

At present 2 Indian sites are listed under it:

★   Keoladeo National Park

In 1993 Chilka lake was also listed in Montreux's record due to the problem of Siltation, But later in 2002, it was removed from the list as a problem tackled by govt actions.

Important Rivers flowing in National Park

Dehing Patkai National Park: It is located in the *Dibrugarh and Tinsukia districts of Assam. It is located in the Dehing patkai landscape which is a lowland rainforest. River Dehing flows through it.*

Anshi National Park: It is a protected area and tiger reserve. *It is located in Karnataka.* The park is a <u>habitat of Bengal Tigers, Black Panthers and Indian Elephants,</u> amongst other distinctive fauna. The Kali River flows through it and is the lifeline of the ecosystem.

Bhitarkanika National Park: It is **located in Odisha.** This national park and wildlife sanctuary is **inundated by the rivers Brahmani, Baitarani, Dhamra, and Pathsala.** It hosts many mangrove species and is the **second-largest mangrove ecosystem** in India.

Asiatic Lion, Cheetah and Elephant

Asiatic Lion can be found only in and around Gir National Park of Gujarat. These are listed as **Endangered Species.** The Asiatic lion is one of five species of cats native to India, along with the Bengal tiger, Indian leopard, snow leopard and clouded leopard.

The Asiatic cheetah is a **Critically Endangered** cheetah subspecies surviving today only in Iran. In 1952 the Asiatic Cheetah was officially declared extinct from India.

The Asian Elephant, also known as the Asiatic elephant, is the only living species of the genus Elephas and is distributed throughout the Indian subcontinent and Southeast Asia, from India in the west, to Nepal in the north, Sumatra in the south, and Borneo in the east. It is *listed as Endangered on the IUCN Red List of threatened species. It is also listed in Schedule I of the Wildlife (Protection) Act, 1992.*

Gahirmatha Sanctuary is a **marine wildlife sanctuary located in Odisha**. It extends from the **Dhamra River mouth in the north to the Brahmani river mouth in the south**. It is very famous for its nesting beach for Olive Ridley Sea Turtles. It is one of the world's most important nesting beaches for turtles.

National Chambal Sanctuary, also called the National Chambal Gharial Wildlife Sanctuary, is a **tri-state protected area** for the protection of the **Critically Endangered gharial,** the red-crowned roof turtle and the Endangered Ganges river dolphin. It is located on the Chambal River near the tripoint of Rajasthan, Madhya Pradesh and Uttar Pradesh.

Vikramshila Sanctuary is the protected area for the **endangered Gangetic Dolphins**. It is **located in Bihar**. The Gangetic Dolphin has been declared the **National Aquatic animal of India**.

Forest (Conservation) Act, 1980

The Forest Conservation Act, 1980 (FCA) is the **principal legislation** that _regulates deforestation in the country._ It prohibits the felling of forests for any "non-forestry" use without prior clearance by the central government.

The clearance process includes seeking consent from local forest rights-holders and wildlife authorities. The Centre is empowered to reject such requests or allow them with legally binding conditions.

In a landmark decision in 1996, the Supreme Court had expanded the coverage of FCA to all areas that satisfied the dictionary definition of a forest; earlier, only lands specifically notified as forests were protected by the enforcement of the FCA.

The FCA is brief legislation with only five sections. _Section 1 defines the extent of coverage of the law, Section 2 restricts activities in forest areas, and the rest deals with the creation of advisory committees, powers of rule-making and penalties._

Bay, Gulf & Strait

A bay is a small body of water or a broad inlet that is set off from a larger body of water generally where the land curves inward. Bays usually occur on oceans, lakes, and gulfs, and generally not on rivers except when there is an artificially enlarged river mouth.

A gulf is a large body of water, sometimes with a narrow mouth, that is almost surrounded by land. It can be considered a large bay. The world's largest gulf is the Gulf of Mexico. The Persian Gulf is important concerning world energy because petroleum is transported through its waters in oil tankers.

A strait is a narrow passageway of water, usually between continents or islands, or between two larger bodies of water. The Strait of Gibraltar is probably the world's most famous strait. It connects the Atlantic Ocean on its west with the Mediterranean Sea on its east. It also separates northern Africa from the Rock of Gibraltar on the southernmost point of the Iberian Peninsula.

Hypoxia

In the ocean and freshwater environments, the term "hypoxia" **refers to low or depleted oxygen in a water body.** Hypoxia is often associated with the overgrowth of certain species of algae, which can lead to oxygen depletion when they die, sink to the bottom, and decompose.

In some cases, **vast stretches of open water become hypoxic.** Unable to sustain life, these areas, **called dead zones, may cause die-offs of fish, shellfish, corals, and aquatic plants.**

The amount of oxygen in any water body varies naturally, both seasonally and over time. This occurs due to a balance between oxygen input from the atmosphere and certain biological and chemical processes, some of which produce oxygen while others consume it.

Stratification in the water column, which occurs when less dense freshwater from an estuary mixes with heavier seawater, is one natural cause of hypoxia. Limited vertical mixing between the water "layers" restricts the supply of oxygen from surface waters to more saline bottom waters, leading to hypoxic conditions in bottom habitats.

Hypoxia occurs most often, however, as a consequence of human-induced factors, especially nutrient pollution (also known as eutrophication). The causes of nutrient pollution, specifically nitrogen and phosphorus nutrients, include agricultural runoff, fossil-fuel burning, and wastewater treatment effluent.

Ekman Spiral

The Ekman spiral is a structure of currents or winds near a horizontal **boundary** in which the flow direction rotates as one moves away from the boundary. **Ekman Spiral is the result of Coriolis force on the movement of surface water.** When surface water molecules move by the force of the wind, they, in turn, drag deeper layers of water molecules below them. Each layer of water molecules is moved by friction from the shallower layer, and each deeper layer moves more slowly than the layer above it until the movement ceases at a depth of about 100 meters (330-feet). Like the surface water, however, **the deeper water is deflected by the Coriolis effect to the right in the Northern Hemisphere and to the left in the Southern Hemisphere.**

As a result, **each successively deeper layer of water moves more slowly to the right or left, creating a spiral effect.** Because the deeper layers of water move more slowly than the shallower layers, **they tend to "twist around" and flow opposite to the surface current.**

Ekman Spiral gives rise to 'Gyres'. These are ocean-swirling currents that occur north and south of the equator. They do not occur at the equator, where the Coriolis Effect is not present.

Ocean Rewilding

Ocean rewilding refers to **reintroducing key plant and animal life into the spaces** they are needed, **allowing them to grow without human interference.**

Ocean rewilding is now **considered to be as crucial and effective as land efforts,** due to the **ocean's innate capabilities to store "blue carbon" in their seagrass meadows, tidal marshes and mangroves.**

It is estimated that the average annual carbon sequestration rate for Mangroves averages between two to four times greater than global rates observed in mature tropical forests.

Marine populations are also served better by ocean rewilding schemes that prevent their ecosystems from devastating human interference. This can include **protections against damaging activities such as trawling and dredging from marine sediments.**

Coral Reefs

Coral reefs are divided into four classes: **fringing reefs, barrier reefs, atolls, and patch reefs.**

Fringing reefs **grow near the coastline around Islands and Continents.** They are separated from the shore by narrow, shallow lagoons. **Fringing reefs are the most common type of reef that we see.**

Barrier reefs are also **parallel to the coastline but are separated by deeper, wider lagoons.** At their shallowest point, they can reach the water's surface forming a "barrier" to navigation. The Great Barrier Reef in Australia is the largest and most famous barrier reef in the world.

Atolls are **rings of Coral** that **create protected lagoons** and are **usually located in the middle of the sea.** Atolls usually **form when islands surrounded by fringing reefs sink into the sea or the sea level rises around them** (these islands are often the tops of underwater volcanoes). **The fringing reefs continue to grow and eventually form circles with lagoons inside.**

Patch reefs are small, **isolated reefs that grow up from the open bottom of the island platform or continental shelf.** They **usually occur between fringing reefs and barrier reefs.** They vary greatly in size, and they rarely reach the surface of the water.

MERPOL Convention

MERPOL Convention **covers pollution of the marine environment by ships from operational or accidental causes.**

It lists various forms of marine pollution caused by oil, noxious liquid substances, harmful substances in packaged form, sewage and garbage from ships, etc.

The Protocol of 1978 was adopted in response to several tanker accidents in 1976–1977.

It is **one of the most important international marine environmental conventions.**

India is a signatory to MARPOL.

Oil Spill in Oceans

An Oil Spill is an accidental/uncontrolled release of crude oil, gasoline, fuels, or other oil by-products into the environment. **Oil spills can pollute land, air, or water, though it is mostly used for oceanic oil spills.**

Various sorbents like straw, volcanic ash, and shavings of polyester-derived plastic that absorb the oil from the water are used.

The National Institute of Ocean Technology (NIOT) has developed an eco-friendly crude oil bioremediation mechanism technology using **consortia (group of two or more species)** of marine microbes **wheat**

bran (WB) immobilized (microbes controlled degradation) on
agro-residue bacterial cells. These hydrocarbon-degrading bacteria
don't depend on hydrocarbon for survival but have a metabolic
mechanism where they use Petroleum products as carbon and energy
source and thus, help clean up oil spills.

Blue Nature Alliance

Blue Nature Alliance is a global partnership. It was **founded and led by
Conservation International, Pew Charitable Trusts, Global Environment
Facility(GEF), Minderoo Foundation and Rob & Melani Walton
Foundation.**

It **aims to**

- ❏ safeguard global ocean biodiversity,
- ❏ build resilience to climate change,
- ❏ promote human well-being and
- ❏ enhance ecosystem connectivity.

The alliance has a target to:

- ➢ *Conserve 18 million square kilometres of ocean in five years.*
- ➢ *Protect 5% of the world's ocean in five years.*
- ➢ *Help the world achieve 30% ocean conservation by 2030.*

The Alliance has started by targeting seven ocean locations. This
includes Antarctica, Fiji, Canada, Seychelles, Palau, the Western Indian
Ocean and Tristan da Cunha, an island in the South Atlantic Ocean.

Forest Rights Act

The Scheduled Tribes and Other Traditional Forest Dwellers (Recognition of Forest Rights) Act, 2006, was passed on 18 December 2006.

The law concerns the rights of forest-dwelling communities to land and other resources, denied to them over decades as a result of the continuance of colonial forest laws in India.

It expands the mandate of the Fifth and the Sixth Schedules of the Constitution that protect the claims of indigenous communities over tracts of land or forests they inhabit.

The act recognizes and vests the forest rights and occupation in **forest land in forest-dwelling Scheduled Tribes (FDST) and Other Traditional Forest Dwellers (OTFD)** who have been residing in such forests for generations. These are:

- Title rights - i.e. ownership - to land that is being farmed by tribals or forest dwellers as of 13 December 2005, subject to a maximum of 4 hectares; ownership is only for land that is being cultivated by the concerned family as on that date, meaning that no new lands are granted.
- Use rights - to minor forest produce (also including ownership), grazing areas, pastoralist routes, etc.
- Relief and development rights - to rehabilitation in case of illegal eviction or forced displacement and basic amenities, subject to restrictions for forest protection.
- Forest management rights - to protect forests and wildlife.

UNESCO

UNESCO is the United Nations Educational, Scientific and Cultural Organization. It seeks to build peace through international cooperation in Education, Sciences and Culture. UNESCO's programmes contribute to the achievement of the Sustainable Development Goals defined in Agenda 2030, adopted by the UN General Assembly in 2015.

Initiatives of UNESCO are:

1. Man and Biosphere Programme: The MAB Programme is an **intergovernmental scientific programme** that <u>aims to establish a scientific basis for enhancing the relationship between people and their environments</u>. It combines the natural and social sciences to improve human livelihoods and safeguard natural and managed ecosystems, thus promoting innovative approaches to economic development that are socially and culturally appropriate and environmentally sustainable.

India has 18 Biosphere reserves out of which 11 have been recognized internationally under Man and Biosphere (MAB) program.

2. International Geoscience and Geoparks Programme: The International Geoscience and Geoparks Programme (IGGP) consists of two pillars:

- **International Geoscience Programme (IGCP), since 1972,** has harnessed the intellectual capacity of a worldwide network of geoscientists to lay the foundation for our planet's future, focusing on responsible and environmental resource extraction, and natural hazards resilience and preparedness, and adaptability in the era of a changing climate.
- **UNESCO Global Geoparks (UGGp)** are laboratories for sustainable development which promote the recognition and management of Earth heritage, and the sustainability of local communities. **As of July 2020, there are 161 UNESCO Global Geoparks within 44 Member States, covering a total area of 325,179 km².**

3. International Hydrological Programme: The Intergovernmental Hydrological Programme (IHP) is the only Intergovernmental programme of the United Nations system devoted to water research and management, and related education and capacity development.

Climate and Clean Air Coalition: *It is an initiative of the United Nations Environment Programme (UNEP). It is the only global effort that unites governments, civil society and the private sector, committed to improving air quality and protecting the climate in the next few decades by reducing short-lived climate pollutants across sectors.*

The Coalition's initial focus is on methane, black carbon, and HFCs. At the same time, partners recognize that action on short-lived climate pollutants must complement and supplement, not replace, global action to reduce carbon dioxide, in particular efforts under the UNFCCC.

Bonn, Vienna, Basel, and Kigali Agreement

Bonn Convention, also known as the **Convention on the Conservation of Migratory Species of Wild Animals** is an international agreement that aims to conserve migratory species throughout their ranges. It is the only global, and United Nations-based, an intergovernmental organization **established exclusively for the conservation and management of terrestrial, aquatic and avian migratory species.**

The Vienna Convention for the Protection of the Ozone Layer is a Multilateral Environmental agreement **signed in 1985** that provided frameworks for international reductions in the production of chlorofluorocarbons due to their contribution to the destruction of the ozone layer, resulting in an increased threat of skin cancer.

Basel Convention is an international treaty that was **designed to reduce the movement of hazardous waste between nations,** and specifically to prevent the transfer of hazardous waste from developed to less developed countries

<u>(LDCs)</u>.

The Kigali Agreement is an **amendment to the Montreal Protocol** which seeks to **gradually reduce the consumption and production of hydrofluorocarbons (HFCs)**. It is a <u>legally binding agreement designed to create rights and obligations in international law</u>.

UNFCCC Annexure

Parties to UNFCCC are classified as:

- **Annexe-I countries: industrialized countries and economies in transition** Annex-I countries which have ratified the Protocol have <u>committed to reducing their emission levels of greenhouse gasses to targets that are mainly set below their 1990 levels.</u> There are 43 Annex-I countries and the European Union is also a member.
- **Annexe-II countries:** developed countries <u>which pay for the costs of developing countries- Annex II countries are a sub-group of the Annex I countries. They comprise the OECD members, excluding those that were economies in transition in 1992.</u>
- **Non-Annex I countries:** <u>Developing countries are not required to reduce emission levels unless developed countries supply enough funding and technology.</u>

<u>**India is a Non-Annex party to UNFCCC.**</u>

<u>**The Wild Life (Protection) Act, 1972**</u> is an Act of the Parliament of India enacted for the protection of plants and animal species.

This Act provides for the protection of the country's **wild animals, birds, and plant species, to ensure environmental and ecological security. Among other things, the Act lays down restrictions on hunting many animal species.**

It has six schedules which give varying degrees of protection:

Schedule I: Under this schedule species need rigorous protection and therefore, the harshest penalties for violation of the law are for species under this Schedule.

Schedule II: Animals under this list are accorded high protection. They cannot be hunted except under threat to human life.

Species listed in Schedule III and Schedule IV are also protected, but the penalties are much lower. **Animals under Schedule V,** e.g. common crows, fruit bats, rats and mice, are legally considered vermin and may be hunted freely.

The specified endemic plants in **Schedule VI are prohibited from cultivation and planting.** These species are:

- Beddomes' cycad (Cycas beddomei)
- Blue Vanda (Vanda soerulec)
- Kuth (Saussurea lappa)
- Ladies slipper orchids (Paphiopedilum spp.)
- Pitcher plant (Nepenthes khasiana)
- Red Vanda (Rananthera inschootiana)

Sundarbans

Sundarbans is a mangrove area in the delta formed by the confluence of the Ganges, Brahmaputra and Meghna Rivers in the Bay of Bengal.

Four protected areas in the Sundarbans are enlisted as UNESCO World Heritage Sites, viz. Sundarbans National Park, Sundarbans West, Sundarbans South and Sundarbans East Wildlife Sanctuaries.

The Sundarbans mangrove ecosystem in India is evaluated as endangered as per IUCN's Red List of Ecosystems framework.

Recently, it was reported by the Zoological Survey of India that out of a total of 1300 species of birds in India 428 species of birds are from Sundarbans. It means that one in every three birds in the country is found in Sundarbans.

Out of 428 birds listed, some, like the **Masked Finfoot and Buffy fish owl,** are recorded only from the Sunderbans. **The area is home to nine out of 12 species of kingfishers** found in the country as well as **rare species such as the Goliath heron and Spoon-billed Sandpiper.**

Countries across the globe committed to creating a new international climate agreement by the conclusion of the U.N. Framework Convention on Climate Change (UNFCCC) Conference of the Parties (COP21) in Paris in December 2015. In preparation, countries have agreed to publicly outline what post-2020 climate actions they intend to take under a new international agreement, known as their Intended Nationally Determined Contributions (INDCs).

India has submitted its Intended Nationally Determined Contribution (INDC) to the United Nations Framework Convention on Climate Change.

Salient features of India's INDC are:

- To put forward and further propagate a healthy and sustainable way of living based on traditions and values of conservation and moderation.
- To adopt a climate-friendly and cleaner path than the one followed hitherto by others at the corresponding level of economic development.
- To reduce the emissions intensity of its GDP by 33 to 35 per cent by 2030 from the 2005 level.
- To achieve about 40 per cent cumulative electric power installed capacity from non-fossil fuel-based energy resources by 2030, with the help of the transfer of technology and low-cost international finance, including from the Green Climate Fund.
- To create an additional carbon sink of 2.5 to 3 billion tonnes of CO_2 equivalent through additional forest and tree cover by 2030.

- To better adapt to climate change by enhancing investments in development programmes in sectors vulnerable to climate change, particularly agriculture, water resources, the Himalayan region, coastal regions, and health and disaster management.
- To mobilize domestic and new and additional funds from developed countries to implement the above mitigation and adaptation actions because of the resource required and the resource gap.
- To build capacities, create a domestic framework and international architecture for quick diffusion of cutting edge climate technology in India and for joint collaborative R&D for such future technologies.

NEST

New and Emerging Strategic Technologies –NEST is created under the Ministry of External Affairs.

The NEST acts as a **nodal point to exchange views with foreign governments on new and emerging strategic technologies.**

The division helps in collaboration with foreign partners in the field of 5G and artificial intelligence.

It helps assess foreign policy and international legal implications of new and emerging technologies and technology-based resources and recommend appropriate foreign policy choice.

The division holds responsibility for matters that involve negotiations with multilateral fora like the United Nations, and G20. This will help to safeguard India's interests as such forums govern the rules of access to such technologies.

Biosparging

Bioremediation is the use of microorganisms to degrade the environmental contaminants into less toxic forms.

Biosparging is an in-situ remediation technology that uses indigenous microorganisms to biodegrade organic constituents in saturated contaminated zones.

Biosparging is the process of groundwater remediation as oxygen, and possible nutrients are injected. When oxygen is injected, indigenous bacteria are stimulated to increase the rate of degradation. Biosparging focuses on saturated contaminated zones, specifically related to groundwater remediation.

Species Recovery Programme

The Species Recovery programme is one of the components of the Integrated Development of Wildlife Habitats' (IDWH).

Started in 2008-09, IDWH is meant for providing support to protected areas, protection of wildlife outside protected areas and recovery programmes for saving critically endangered species and habitats.

So far, the recovery programme for critically endangered species in India includes 22 wildlife species.

The species are: These are the Snow Leopard, Bustard (including Floricans), Dolphin, Hangul, Nilgiri Tahr, Marine Turtles, Dugongs, Caracal, Edible Nest Swiftlet, Asian Wild Buffalo, Nicobar Megapode, Manipur Brow-antlered Deer, Vultures, Malabar Civet, Indian Rhinoceros, Asiatic Lion, Swamp Deer, Jerdon's Courser, the Northern River Terrapin, Clouded Leopard, Arabian Sea Humpback Whale and Red Panda.

Department of Biotechnology (DBT)

The Department of Biotechnology (DBT) was set up in February 1986.

First Secretary was Dr S. Ramachandran. **It works under the Ministry of Science and Technology, Government of India.**

Functions:

Promotes the biotech industry. Promotes large scale use of Biotechnology. Supports R&D and manufacturing in Biology. Identifies and sets up Centres of Excellence for R&D.

Develops an integrated programme for Human Resource Development (HRD). Serves as Nodal Point for specific International Collaborations. Establishes infrastructure facilities to support R&D and production. Evolves biosafety guidelines, manufacture and application of cell-based vaccines. **Serve as a nodal point for the collection and dissemination of information relating to biotechnology.**

Genome India Initiative: Approved in 2020. It involves the scanning of 20,000 Indian genomes to develop diagnostic tests and effective therapies for treating diseases such as cancer.

Two phases of the programme:

1. The first phase of the project involves sequencing the complete genomes of 10,000 healthy Indians.
2. The second phase involves genome sequencing of 10,000 diseased individuals.

National Centre for Cell Sciences will collect samples of the microbiome from the human gut. Data on genome sequencing would be accessible to researchers through National Biological Data Centre envisaged in Biological Data Storage, Access and Sharing Policy.

State of Environment Report, 2022 (Highlights)

The Centre for Science and Environment (CSE) released the State of

Environment Report, 2022.

The CSE is a public interest research and advocacy organisation based in New Delhi, India. It researches into, lobbies for and communicates the urgency of development that is both sustainable and equitable.

There are 14 chapters in the report that covers the pandemic, sustainable development goals, poverty, energy, rural development, etc.

The report states that <u>"India is all set to usher in a 'pandemic generation', with 375 million children (from newborns to 14-year-olds) likely to suffer long-lasting impacts, ranging from being underweight, stunting (low height-for-age) and increased child mortality, to losses in education and work productivity"</u>.

The report also charts how pollution levels have increased. India's air, water and land have become more polluted between 2009 and 2018.

The report carries a special section on the state of the Indian states, particularly on their performance on Sustainable Development Goals (SDG). India ranked 117 among 192 nations in terms of sustainable development and was now behind all South Asian nations except Pakistan.

Best Performing States: Kerala, Himachal Pradesh, Andhra Pradesh, Tamil Nadu and Telangana.
Worst Performing States: Bihar, Jharkhand, Arunachal Pradesh, Meghalaya and Uttar Pradesh.
No state was found to be on track to meet all the SDGs by 2030.

Birdlife International

BirdLife International is a global partnership of non-governmental organizations (NGOs) that strives to conserve birds and their habitats.

It is an accredited organization of the United Nations Environment Programme (UNEP).

BirdLife International's priorities include preventing the extinction of bird species, identifying and safeguarding important sites for birds, maintaining and restoring key bird habitats, and empowering conservationists worldwide.

BirdLife International has identified 13,000 Important Bird and Biodiversity Areas and is the **official International Union for Conservation of Nature's Red List authority for birds.**

BirdLife International has established that 1,375 bird species (13% of the total) are threatened with extinction (critically endangered, endangered or vulnerable).

Bombay Natural History Society (BNHS)

It is one of the **largest non-governmental organisations in India** engaged in conservation and biodiversity research.

It is the **partner of BirdLife International in India. It has been designated as a 'Scientific and Industrial Research Organisation' by the Department of Science and Technology.**

Many prominent naturalists, including the ornithologists Sálim Ali and S. Dillon Ripley, have been associated with it.

The Asian waterbird census is an annual exercise undertaken in India by the Bombay Natural History Society in association with Wetlands International, in which enthusiastic birdwatchers count the birds by observing them near their respective breeding grounds. **The exercise is a part of the 'International waterbird census',** an international exercise. It also **aims to create awareness**

regarding bird species as well as the health of the wetlands, which are facing severe threats amidst anthropogenic disturbance. It is **conducted in January every year.**

Key Biodiversity Areas (KBA)

Key Biodiversity Areas (KBAs) are <u>nationally identified sites that contribute significantly to the global persistence of biodiversity, in terrestrial, freshwater and marine ecosystems</u>.

The **identification of KBAs** is an **important approach to address biodiversity conservation** at the site scale i.e. at the level of individual protected areas.

In 2016, the International Union for the Conservation of Nature (IUCN) published a Global Standard for the Identification of Key Biodiversity Areas 1, providing criteria under which an area can be quantitatively assessed for inclusion as a Key Biodiversity Area, with the thresholds being applicable and comparable across taxonomic groups.

KBA identification should build off the existing network of KBAs, which includes:

- Important Bird and Biodiversity Areas (IBAs)
- Important Plant Areas (IPAs)
- Important Sites for Freshwater Biodiversity
- Alliance for Zero Extinction (AZE) sites

KBAs can be used to support the strategic expansion of protected area networks by governments and civil society working towards the achievement of the Aichi Biodiversity Targets (in particular Targets 11 and 12) as established by the Convention on Biological Diversity.

IUCN identifies 531 KBA sites in India but these have no legal basis.

Conservation Reserves

Conservation reserves and community reserves are terms denoting protected areas of the country which typically act as buffer zones or connectors and migration corridors between established National Parks, Wildlife Sanctuaries and Reserved and Protected forests. Such areas are designated as conservation areas if they are uninhabited and completely owned by the Government of India (GoI) but used for subsistence by communities, and community areas if part of the lands are privately owned.

These protected area categories were **first introduced in the Wildlife (Protection) Amendment Act of 2002 – the amendment to the Wildlife Protection Act of 1972.**

These categories were added because of reduced protection in and around existing or proposed protected areas due to private ownership of land, and land use.

Tiruvidaimarudur Conservation Reserve declared on **February 14, 2005**, is the First Conservation Reserve to be established in the country.

The Dr KK Mohammed Koya Sea Cucumber Conservation Reserve is the **first sea cucumber conservation area** in the world. **It is located in the Cheriyapani Reef in the Indian Union Territory of Lakshadweep. It was formed in 2020. It covers an area of 239 km2.**

In India, the **sea cucumber is protected under Schedule I of the Wildlife Protection Act, 1972,** according to which the sea cucumbers cannot be transported for commercial use. **In 2002, the Environmental Ministry of India banned the commercial harvesting of sea cucumbers.**

National Parks & Wildlife Sanctuaries

The Wildlife (Protection) Act, 1972 provides for the establishment of Protected Areas in India. There are different categories of protected areas which are managed with different objectives for the larger motive of conservation.

National Parks:

National parks _protect the entire ecosystem, that is, flora, fauna, landscape, etc. of that region._ The national parks not only conserve wildlife but also provide a diversion of environmental and landscape heritage in a manner that does not harm it, to provide enjoyment to future generations.

National parks are given a greater degree of protection, with human activity greatly restricted. Only certain areas can be visited and **only activities permitted by the chief wildlife warden of the State** are allowed in the park.

Wildlife Sanctuaries:

Wildlife Sanctuary, as the name implies, is a place that is _reserved exclusively for wildlife use_, which includes animals, reptiles, insects, birds, etc. wild animals, especially those in danger of extinction and the rare ones, so that they can live in peace for a lifetime and keep their population viable. Restrictions are less and open to visitations by the general public.

Wildlife is the main natural heritage, worldwide. Continuous industrialisation and deforestation have posed a threat of extinction to wildlife. Wildlife sanctuaries refer to an area that provides protection and living conditions favourable to wild animals. India has 553 wildlife sanctuaries.

Intertropical Convergence Zone (ITCZ)

The Inter-Tropical Convergence Zone (ITCZ) is a **low-pressure zone located at the equator** where **trade winds converge**, and so, it is a **zone where air tends to ascend.**

In July, the **ITCZ is located around 20°N-25°N latitudes** (over the Gangetic plain), sometimes called the monsoon trough.

This monsoon trough encourages the development of thermal low over North and North-West India. Due to the shift of ITCZ, the trade winds of the southern hemisphere cross the equator between 40° and 60°E longitudes and start blowing from southwest to northeast due to the Coriolis force. It becomes a southwest monsoon.

In winter, the ITCZ moves southward, and so the reversal of winds from northeast to south and southwest takes place. They are called northeast monsoons.

National Bureau of Soil Survey Entisols, Vertisols, and Aridisols

The National Bureau of Soil Survey and the Land Use Planning Institute under the control of the **Indian Council of Agricultural Research (ICAR)** did a lot of studies on Indian soils. In their effort to study soil and to make it comparable at the international level, the ICAR has classified the Indian soils based on their nature and character as per the **United States Department of Agriculture (USDA) Soil Taxonomy.**

Entisols are immature soils that lack the vertical development of horizons. These soils are often associated with recently deposited sediments from wind, water or ice erosion.

Vertisols are heavy clay soils that show significant expansion and contraction due to the presence or absence of moisture. These are common in areas that have shale parent material and heavy precipitation.

Aridisols soils develop in very dry environments.

According to ICAR in India major area (39.74%) comes under the Inceptisol soils which are young soils that are more developed than entisols.